# Paleo Diet

*Essentials Anti-Inflammatory Diet and Expanded Paleo*

*for Beginners and Seniors Dieters*

**Roland O. Denis**

# Table of Contents

# INTRODUCTION

Are you the type that whenever you look at yourself in the mirror you get discourage due to the shape of your body and desperately in need of help to lose weight and feel more motivated during the day and also get fit just like your pairs?

Most other diet books give you a regimen then leave you to fend for yourself, Paleo Diet Cookbook is your one-stop guide for feeling healthy, losing weight, and increasing your energy level. By focusing on low-carb, high-protein meals that remove all processed foods. Paleo Diet cookbook will help decrease your odds of developing common health ailments such as diabetes, hypertension, heart disease, and more.

# CHAPTER 1

## What's the Paleo Diet?

Importantly, the Paleo diet is a method of eating that's much like how historical human beings ate. Quite simply, if our celebrated forefathers could search or collect it, we can (and really should) consume it.

The concept behind that is that the "contemporary diet plan" continues to be influenced by agricultural and commercial industries to add foods that aren't the majority of appropriate, organic, or healthy options, by "getting back to our roots" having a diet plan that includes organic, unrefined foods, we can provide our anatomies optimal nutrition and health.

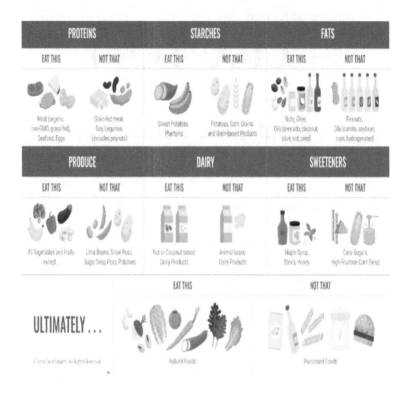

| PROTEINS | | STARCHES | | FATS | |
|---|---|---|---|---|---|
| EAT THIS | NOT THAT | EAT THIS | NOT THAT | EAT THIS | NOT THAT |
| Meat (organic, non-GMO, grass-fed), Seafood, Eggs | Grain-fed meat, Soy, Legumes (includes peanuts) | Sweet Potatoes, Plantains | Potatoes, Corn, Grains and Grain-based Products | Nuts, Ghee, Oils (avocado, coconut, olive, nut, seed) | Peanuts, Oils (canola, soybean, corn, hydrogenated) |

| PRODUCE | | DAIRY | | SWEETENERS | |
|---|---|---|---|---|---|
| EAT THIS | NOT THAT | EAT THIS | NOT THAT | EAT THIS | NOT THAT |
| All Vegetables and Fruits except ... | Lima Beans, Snow Peas, Sugar Snap Peas, Potatoes | Nut or Coconut-based Dairy Products | Animal-based Dairy Products | Maple Syrup, Stevia, Honey | Cane Sugars, High-Fructose Corn Syrup |

| EAT THIS | NOT THAT |
|---|---|
| Natural Foods | Processed Foods |

ULTIMATELY . . .

## *Paleo Meals Listing: What things to Eat and What Never to Eat*

When trying to adhere to a "caveman diet plan," mainly because of what you may expect, presently, there are a lot of food items that limit you, especially the ones that are sugary, refined, or excessively processed. Therefore to make slicing through the what-can-I-have mess as simple as possible, here's a fast insight at everything you can and can't consume on the Paleo diet plan:

What to eat about paleo:

- *Fruit.* Plums, pears, grapefruits, etc.

- *Nut products.* Macadamias, walnuts, pecans, etc.

- *Veggies.* Broccoli, spinach, tomato vegetables, etc.

- *Seed products.* Sunflower, pumpkin, pomegranate, etc.

- *Protein.* Pig, eggs, meat, seafood, chicken, crazy sport, etc.

- *Healthful Fat.* Essential olive oil, essential coconut oil, grass-fed butter, ghee, lard, etc.

What you should never eat in paleo:

- *Some dairy products.* Dairy, parmesan cheese, sour lotion, yogurt, lotion, etc. Milk products such as grass-fed butter and ghee are usually permitted on Paleo.

- *Dried beans.* Nuts (and peanut butter), soy, navy blue coffee beans, dark-eyed peas, kidney coffee beans, pinto coffee beans, etc.

- *Grains.* Whole wheat, oats, rye, hammer toe, barley, brownish grain, bread breadcrumbs, etc.

- *Ready-made oils.* Canola essential oil, essential veggie oil, margarine, etc.

- *Sugary snack foods and beverages.* Soda pops, some fruit drinks, packed snacks, etc.

- *Whitened potatoes.* Some claim that, in moderation, whitened taters are usually suitable to eat on the Paleo diet plan, while some state to prevent them.

## *Paleo Alternatives Manual and Infographic*

Right now, guess what happens to food items that are on/off the desk, you're one stage nearer to Paleo achievement! Below, we've compiled a summary of off-limits meals showing you how to exchange them for great tasting Paleo-friendly choices creatively. For pure research, print the useful infographic below to have in your kitchen or kitchen area!

BEANS — Vegetables chopped small (mushrooms, carrots, bell peppers, etc.) — Proteins (chicken, eggs, etc)

EDAMAME — Green beans, chopped — Vegetables chopped small (broccoli, bok choy, peas, etc.)

The good news concerning the Paleo diet is the fact that since it targets simple whole foods, most of the ingredients you'll need can be found at your local supermarket or farmer's market; you don't need to include a large amount of specialized ingredient to your kitchen.

But you might have problems searching for something you choose to possess, we recommend looking into internet vendors like Thrive Market to fill up an alternative in addition to accessible Paleo components like bone tissue broth, avocado mayonnaise, and coconut aminos.

## *White Colored Spud Alternatives For Paleo*

Like we mentioned previously, white taters certainly are a bit controversial. Whether you take them in or not, here are things to make use of if you want an alternative:

- Sweet potatoes

- Cauliflower

- Turnips

- Celeriac

## *Dairy Products Alternatives For Paleo*

There are always a ton of dairy-totally free products available in the market, from yogurt to milk, that produce swapping away dairy for Paleo alternatives fast and straightforward. Here are things to make use of if you want a Paleo dairy products alternative:

- *Yogurt and sour lotion.* Coconut yogurt or almond yogurt.

- *Lotion.* Coconut lotion or cashew lotion.

- *Parmesan cheese.* Cashew mozzarella cheese or dietary candida.

- *Whole milk.* Coconut dairy or enthusiast milk (cashew, macadamia, almond).

## Feed, Carb, And Legume Alternatives For Paleo

The USDA's Foods Pyramid Guideline recommends eating 6 to 11 servings of cereal, bread, pasta, or rice each day - the biggest meal of any food group. Around the Paleo diet plan, it's zero. Mix that without dried beans, and you'll get almost all demanding support beams of Paleo. Fortunately, there are a few innovative options. Here're things to make use of if you want a replacement:

- *Hammer's toe.* Tomatoes or veggies cut little (mushrooms, celery, bell peppers).

- *Noodles or pasta.* Spiralized vegetable noodles (zucchini, sweet spud, butternut lead pages, carrot), spaghetti lead capture pages, kelp noodles, or shirataki (yam) noodles.

- *Grain.* Cauliflower grain or plantains.

- *Flour.* Coconut flour, almond flour, arrowroot natural powder, or tapioca flour.

- *Breadcrumbs.* Flax food, chia seed products, floor pepitas, surface nut products, almond flour.

- *Tortillas.* Coconut-centered tortillas, lettuce, or cabbage wraps.

- *Pizzas brown crust area.* Cauliflower brown crust area, portobello mushrooms, zucchini vessels, Italian language eggplant sliced up into models, or lovely taters chopped up into times.

- *Coffee beans.* Veggies cut little (mushrooms, celery, bell peppers) or protein like poultry and eggs.

- *Edamame.* Chopped natural coffee beans or veggies cut little (broccoli, bok choy, peas).

- *Nuts.* Cashews, pistachios, pinus radiata nut products, or walnuts.

*Notice:* Whole wheat gluten is frequently found in food items you'll never expect to think it is inside. Therefore it's a good concept to check out your meal brands when you're simply starting the Paleo diet plan to prevent whole wheat chemicals and sneaky soy.

## Flavor And Condiment Paleo Substitutes

- Canola or soybean essential oil. Avocado essential oil, essential coconut oil, essential olive oil, grass-fed butter, or Ghee.

- Soy spices. Coconut Aminos.

- Sugars.* Maple syrup, darling, stevia.

- Peanut butter. Almond butter, sunflower seeds butter, or cashew butter.

*Notice: Although some Paleo elements overlap using the whole-30 diet plan, added sugars, still organic choices such as maple syru*

*p and darling, aren't whole-30 compliant.*

## *Paleo Treat Substitutes*

To avoid eating non-Paleo meals when you're hungry, it's a good thing to keep several snack foods readily available. Here's what things to make use of:

- **Spud Potato chips.** Kale potato chips, brussels sprout potato chips, or plantain potato chips.

- **German fries.** Lovely spud french fries, parsnip french fries, or carrot french fries.

- **Granola.** Enthusiast blend.

- **Crackers.** Vegetable crudites.

- *Mozzarella cheese or even drop.* Baba ganoush, roasting reddish pepper spices, or coconut yogurt with lime and natural herbs.

## Pasta, Taco, And Hamburger Paleo Substitutes

Eliminating well-known foods that want tacos and hamburgers could be a concern. Rather than eliminating them from your diet plan completely, get innovative with the method for you to develop them. Can't consume a taco covering? Work with a lettuce leaf like a cover rather. Below are a few suggestions to allow you to get started:

- *Pasta meals.* Gown spices over chicken white meat, cut veggies (zucchini, cauliflower, turnips, mushrooms, cabbage) into pasta size and make use of the same spices, or work with a spiralizer to create vegetable noodles (zucchini, special taters, celery, turnips).

- *Tacos.* Work with a lettuce leaf or perhaps a cabbage cover, take pleasure in filling up over a cooked sweet spud, or become burrito dishes by helping toppings over cauliflower grain.

- *Hamburgers.* Function patty more than a mattress of combined vegetables, covered in lettuce, or higher roasting portobello mushrooms. Or, terrain meats function more than a cooked sweet spud.

# CHAPTER 2

## Paleo, Atkins, And Keto Are Low-Carb Diet Programs, Thus What's The Distinction?

Other than removing almost all our carbs will the Atkins, Paleo, and keto diet plans be at the same point? Brief answer - zero.

Although each one of these diets is low-carb, each of them serves various purposes. We've divided the facts of three well-known low-carb diet programs below. Many of these diet plans can lead to excess weight reduction, however, the one that is right for you depends on your general objectives.

America Department of Agriculture and Department of

Health Insurance and Human Service's Diet recommendations advise that adults split up their consumption of calories into 45 to 65 percent carbs, 10 to 35 percent protein, and 20 to 35 percent fat. Before starting these, it's recommended that you check on your doctor for consultation.

## *What's the ketogenic diet plan?*

Much better referred to as keto, the dietary plan has been created in the 1920s to deal with epilepsy. Vintage keto needs that 90% of someone's calorie consumption result from excess fat, 6% from proteins, and 4 % from carbs.

You can find different variations of the dietary plan on the market, and all are saturated in fat and lower in carbs, although they range between 60 to 90% of the dietary plan via fat.

The goal of the keto diet plan would be to force your body to get into ketosis, which is a metabolic declare that uses fat for energy rather than glucose (carbs). To get into ketosis, people have to be consuming less than 50 grams of carbs each day for a couple of times.

Even though diet is low-carb, its focus is usually to be saturated in fat with quite a few proteins - but mainly fat. You can find no limitations on the sort of extra fat you're likely to eat. Therefore fans of keto are usually advised to eat things such as bacon, avocados, and butter.

Keto leans around the stricter part of low-carb diet programs as you must maintain a firm nutrition strategy, which means that your whole body may successfully get into ketosis.

### What's the paleo diet plan?

The paleo diet plan demands followers to return to just

how individuals were eating through the Paleolithic era, 2.6 million years back, eating just like a hunter-gatherer.

Paleo concentrates mostly on the high-protein diet plan with plenty of fruit and veggies. Unlike keto and Atkins, the dietary plan does not try to be low-carb; it is merely due to the meals it slashes out, which includes grains, dairy products, dried beans, and processed food items.

While keto won't discriminate between what forms of fat you need to consume, the paleo diet plan advises individuals to avoid particular sorts of natural oils and trans body fat. And though it is possible to consume all of the peanut butter you need on the keto diet plan, the paleo diet plan slashes out peanut butter because theoretically nuts are usually categorized as dried beans. The primary focus of paleo would be to get visitors to get back to eating like our hunter-gatherer ancestors.

# What's the Atkins diet plan?

The dietary plan is specifically marketed and called a low-carb diet. You can find two editions from the Atkins diet plan right now, Atkins 20, which is the initial, and Atkins 40, which is a strategically designed for those seeking to lose significantly less than 40 lbs.

The classic Atkins diet plan has four phases - the initial phase starts with having people eating 20 to 25 grams of carbs each day and slowly progresses to phase four, where people are allowed 80 to 100 grams of carbs, which is nevertheless considered low-carb.

Atkins also targets internet carbs. Rather than keeping track of all carbs because the dietary plan puts dietary fiber and sugar into consideration, whereas paleo and keto avoid. Therefore if an item offers 10 grams of carbs, but 3 grams of dietary fiber, and 1 gram of sugars, after that, your online carbs will be 6 grams.

And while it is possible to prepare diet-friendly foods at home, Atkins gives pre-packaged and processed items that meet up with the eating requirements.

Paleo and keto usually do not offer you items that involve Atkins; thus fans are anticipated to adhere to the recommendations independently.

# CHAPTER 3

## What's the Distinction Between Paleo and Whole-30?

The Whole-30 and paleo diet programs are two of the very most popular eating patterns. Both promote whole or minimally processed food items and shun processed items abundant with added sugar, body fat, and sodium. Furthermore, both guarantee to help you to shed weight and enhance your general wellness.

### *What's the paleo diet plan?*

The paleo diet plan is patterned after what human hunter-gatherer ancestors could have eaten, the fact remains that these foods drive back contemporary illnesses.

Therefore, it's predicated on the whole, minimally processed food items and promises to help you shed weight without keeping track of calories from fat.

**Food items to consume:** meats, seafood, eggs, fruit, veggies, nut products, seed products, natural herbs, spices or herbs, and certain veggie natural oils, such as coconut or more virgin essential olive oil - also, wines and chocolates in smaller amounts

**Meals to avoid:** processed food items, added glucose, artificial sweeteners, trans excess fat, grains, dairy products, dried beans, plus some natural veggie oils, including soybean, sunflower, and safflower oil

Furthermore, you're encouraged to select grass-fed and natural products whenever possible.

### What's the Whole30 diet plan?

The Whole30 diet plan is a month-long program made to

reset your metabolism and reshape your relationship with food. Like paleo, it promotes whole foods and promises to help you to shed weight without keeping track of unhealthy calories.

The dietary plan also aims to improve your energy amounts, enhance your sleep, reduce urges, heighten your athletic performance, and help you in identifying food intolerances.

**Food items to consume:** meats, chicken, seafood, eggs, fruit, veggies, nut products, seed products, and some extra fat, such as herb natural oils, duck body fat, clarified butter, and ghee

**Meals to avoid:** added sugar, artificial sweeteners, processed chemicals, alcoholic beverages, grains, dairy products, and pulses and dried beans, including soy.

After the very first thirty days, you're permitted to slowly reintroduced limited foods - individually - to check your tolerance in their mind. Those food items which you tolerate nicely may end up being added back to your regular.

## *What exactly are their similarities and variations?*

The Whole30 and paleo diet plans have become similar in their restrictions and health effects but diverge in their implementation.

**Both cut right out precisely the same food groups.**

Nutrient-rich fruits & vegetables are usually abundant in the paleo and Whole30 diets.

Having said that, both diet programs curb your consumption of grains, dairy products, and dried beans, which present a range of beneficial nutrients, such as dietary fiber, carbs, proteins, metal, magnesium, selenium, and many nutritional vitamins.

Trimming these food types from your diet plan seems to lessen your carbohydrate consumption while improving your protein usage while you start counting on a lot more high-protein meals.

Nevertheless, low-carb, high-protein diet plans may not be suitable for everyone, including sports athletes who require an increased carb intake. A higher proteins intake could also get worse problems for those who are usually vulnerable to kidney gemstones or have kidney disease.

What's even more, thoroughly limiting your intake of grains, dairy products, and dried beans could make it more challenging to fulfill all your every day nutritional requirements.

**Both aid weight reduction**

Because of the restrictive character, both diet programs

might create the caloric debt you will need to lose excess weight without requiring you to gauge servings or even count numbers of calories definitely

What's even more, paleo and Whole30 are usually abundant with fibrous fruits & vegetables. Diet programs saturated in dietary fiber might help decrease food cravings and desires while advertising emotions of fullness - which might help you shed weight

Furthermore, by eliminating grains, dairy products, and legumes, these eating designs are reduced carbs and higher in proteins than the typical diet plan.

High-protein diet plans tend to naturally lessen your hunger and help you in maintaining muscle size while losing weight, which are fundamental aspects of weight reduction

Having said that, paleo and Whole30 could be challenging to keep up with due to these limitations. Unless your meal options on these diet programs turn out to be a routine, you're most likely to gain the weight you dropped once you set off the diet

**Both might promote similar health advantages**

Paleo and Whole30 might provide comparable health advantages. This can be because they're abundant with vegetables & fruits and discourage ready-made foods which are often loaded with sugar, fat, or salt.

Appropriately, studies show that paleo diet improved insulin sensitivity and reduced inflammation and blood sugar - just all factors which might reduce your threat of type 2 diabetes.

This diet could also lower risk factors for cardiovascular disease, including blood circulation pressure, triglycerides, and LDL (bad) cholesterol levels. Even though the Whole30 diet hasn't been as extensively researched, it could offer virtually identical health benefits because of its resemblance to paleo.

**Might vary in concentration and sustainability**

Although both diets try to help you shed weight and enhance your health, they differ within their focus. For example, Whole30 states to help you identify feasible food intolerances, requiring you to cut right out slightly, even more foods compared to the paleo diet plan - at the very least.

Also, Whole30's preliminary stage is maintained simply for one month. After, it gets substantially less restrictive, letting you progressively reintroduce restricted food items if the body tolerates them.

Alternatively, the paleo diet plan appears more lenient. For example, it enables smaller amounts of wines and chocolates from the starting point. Nevertheless, its set of limited meals continues to be the same, whether you abide by it for four weeks or 12 months.

Just like, some individuals discover that Whole30 diet plan is a lot more difficult to check out initially but better to stay with on the long-phrase. Nonetheless, the chance of leaving the dietary plan may be higher in Whole30 because it's so rigid in advance.

The Whole30 and paleo diet plans are similarly structured around whole foods and provide comparable benefits, including weight reduction.

That been said, they could furthermore curb your chemical consumption and become difficult to sustain. While Whole30 is initially stricter, its very first stage is time-limited and quickly helps reduce its limitations. In the meantime, paleo maintains the same restrictions throughout. If you're interested in these diet plans, you can test them both to find out which is most effective for you.

# CHAPTER 4

## Keto Diet Plan Vs Paleo Diet Plan: Is Keto Much Better Than Paleo?

If you want to enhance your wellness or lose a few pounds, you would have heard about the ketogenic diet plan and paleo diet plan before. Given that they both restrict a number of the same meals organizations, lots of people will blend them up, considering the fact that they offer the same advantages.

The difference between both of these diet programs, nevertheless, plays a far more significant role than you might think. Keto on a diet, for instance, was created to allow you to get into ketosis, as the paleo diet plan just eliminates particular foods groupings from your dish.

That one distinction is all that it requires to provide each diet its benefits and drawbacks. To help you to find out what diet strategy will be most excellent for you let's have a nearer, take a look at both means of consuming.

## The Ketogenic Diet

The keto diet plan was initially intended to help children control and reduce the outward symptoms of epilepsy. The initial purpose behind the dietary plan has been to make a pseudo-fasting reaction that transmits your body into dietary ketosis without leading to severe nutritional insufficiencies.

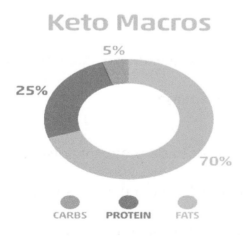

This is a simple diagram that provides you with the normal macronutrient runs from the keto diet plan:

- As you can see, the macronutrient we restrict with keto is carbs. In so doing, we get our anatomy's primary gas resource aside and pressure it to adapt by losing fat and ketones for energy.

- Due to following this method of feeding, lots of people with epilepsy could decrease the severity and frequency of these seizures. Also, ketones (the gasoline that we burn off when we take in ketosis), as well as the keto diet plan, had been discovered to possess numerous results on your body, which include enhanced psychological clearness and hunger decrease.

- With one of these promising discoveries came more study on what keto dieting and ketones might help people who have common conditions, like cancer,

Alzheimer's disease, type 2 diabetes, and obesity, as well. Nevertheless, typically the most popular advantage that carb limitation is well known for the excess fat reduction.

## *Keto For Weight Loss*

As a weight loss device, the ketogenic diet plan is undoubtedly probably one of the most effective nourishment applications on the market. The key reason why they have a spectacular impact on your body for weight loss is that it suppresses appetite and helps prevent overeating in a range of methods.

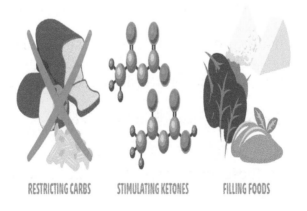

RESTRICTING CARBS    STIMULATING KETONES    FILLING FOODS

The keto diet produces a trifecta of lasting results by:

- **Limiting carbohydrates.** By eliminating the carbs, we cut right out a few of all palatable food items that trigger us to overeat and put on weight.

- **Revitalizing ketone manufacturing.** Whenever you adhere to the keto diet plan, you will find yourself burning up more ketones instead of sugars. Ketones have already been discovered to suppress the urge for food.

- **Prioritizing filling up meals.** Proteins and dietary fiber will be the two nearly all satiating nutrition we can possess, and several meals that individuals consume on keto could have one, another, or both in them. Also, several individuals discover fat meals as immensely satisfying as nicely.

Altogether these three aspects result in keto people to

sense fuller often and eat fewer calorie consumption. This is the principal reason keto offers excess weight reduction for many individuals.

Nevertheless, let's remember concerning the Paleo diet. Though it is not precisely like the keto diet plan, it nevertheless gets the possibility to boost wellness and whole body structure significantly.

## The Paleo Diet

The Paleo diet plan grew to become popularized because of the diet plan that people had developed to consume. What precisely will this imply?

There is a great deal of discussion on this topic, which leads to a variety of iterations from the Paleo diet plan. Nevertheless, what most Paleo individuals acknowledge will be that people should cut out  (or at the very least control) food items that originated from the farming period (milk products, grains, glucose, dried beans, prepared natural oils, etc.).

Generally, the Paleo diet primarily includes top-quality meat, seafood, veggies, and fruits while restricting dairy products, feed, legume, and processed oil intake. The principal concentrate from the Paleo diet plan will be on foods that are high in quality (not the amount), eliminating the "harmful" and changing it using the "healthful."

One of the primary benefits of this process is that it includes an abundance of health advantages without forcing you to revolve your way of life around incredibly strict chemical proportions. Just by replacing paleo-approved meals for the food items that arrived directly after we start creating materials and domesticating creatures, you'll, in theory, have the ability to consume like our forefathers and enhance your wellness.

You can even use this eating approach like a pseudo-elimination diet plan which allows you to learn if you're allergic or even sensitive to common meals (whole wheat, and dairy products) - or it is possible to drop back on Paleo in-take when the keto diet plan is not the proper diet plan for you.

## Producing A Good Choice: If You Adhere To Paleo Or Even Keto?

The choice between your Paleo diet plan and a ketogenic diet plan shouldn't be taken lightly. Both weight loss programs will need severe dedication - in the end; they need to eliminate several palatable and available food items. However, in their methods, both diet plans will help you shed weight and enhance your wellness.

To make it easier for you to decide, let's have a look at the deal-breakers for every diet plan.

## *When Keto Is not Best For You*

Even though the keto diet might help with various conditions, it isn't the very best diet for everybody. People who have thyroid problems or even familial hypercholesterolemia, for instance, might battle to stay healthy while restricting carbs.

Simply because an individual yielded incredible outcomes through the use of keto does not mean it's the finest option for you. If you opt to attempt a dietary plan for yourself, be sure you are always mindful of your health insurance and what you experience with this method of consumption.

After one or two weeks of keto dieting, you'll be able to

determine if keto is best for you. If your wellbeing diminishes following the keto flu signs and symptoms move, it might cost much better having a diet plan, like the Paleo diet plan, that will be increased in carbs than keto.

## *When Paleo Is not Best For You*

Paleo is near while challenging to check out keto. Removing all grains, dairy products, dried beans, prepared essential oil, and sugar for the diet plan is usually hard - particularly when you consider the truth that they are usually the very best resources of calorie consumption in the western community.

Moreover, you might find yourself passing up on some vitamins and nutrients that a lot of people get from your foods that paleo statements are not healthful. This can result in particular nutritional insufficiencies that caused the phase for health problems.

Another downside of Paleo is usually that you'll not go through the great things about ketosis. The keto diet plan is a diet plan which allows you to maintain ketosis and never have to quick.

## *Advantages And Disadvantages Of Paleo And Keto*

This is a fast overview of the advantages and drawbacks of every diet plan:

### *Benefits of the Ketogenic Diet*

- Slashes out many unhealthy foods

- Reduces calorie consumption without growing hunger

- Encourages sustained ketosis in a wholesome way

- Offers us all the advantages of burning up ketones for fuel

- Able to encourage constant weight reduction

- It may be used to significantly help individuals who have diabetes, malignancy, cognitive disability, and epilepsy, in addition to a great many other conditions

- Help reduce chronic inflammation

***Disadvantages from the Ketogenic Diet***

- Must be strict with carb intake to check out properly

- Requires you to monitor your macros for ideal results

- Slashes out some of the most enjoyable foods

- Could cause adverse hormone changes and/or harmful cholesterol level in a few people

- Hard to adjust to for many individuals.

- Impairs many areas of high-intensity workout performance

- Results in you been susceptible to quite a few supplement and nutrient deficiencies

### *Benefits of the Paleo Diet*

- Follows simple rules.

- Replaces processed food items with healthier meals that are usually a lot more satiating.

- Can make it better to maintain the caloric debt and shed weight and never have to monitor calories.

- May improve general metabolic health insurance and help reduce the severe nature of numerous normal problems such as cardiovascular disease and Type 2 diabetes.

- Offers people with plenty of carbs to keep up high-intensity workout performance.

- Help reduce chronic inflammation.

- We can reduce carb consumption without provoking keto flu signs and symptoms or even adverse hormone changes.

### *Disadvantages from the Paleo Diet*

- Could be challenging to implement.

- Slashes out many enjoyable foods.

- Can lead to a deficiency in a few minerals and vitamins.

- Might require you to monitor macros for the very best results.

Here's a Venn diagram to make it simpler to see the variations and similarities between your two diet programs:

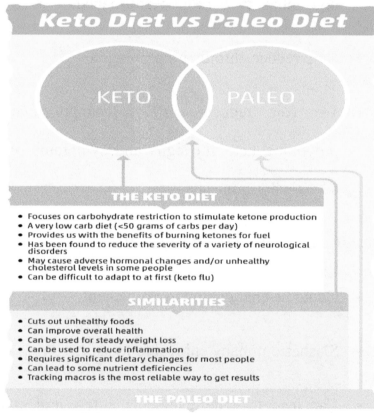

Whether you select Paleo or keto depends on your objectives, your wellbeing, your way of life, as well as your meal atmosphere. If you wish to enjoy the advantages of ketosis, for instance, keto may be the strategy to use.

In contrast, for anybody who would want to cut right out particular food groups without rigidly limiting carbs, after that Paleo will undoubtedly be ideal for you.

Generally, if your present diet plan option does not help you in meeting up with your targets while increasing your wellbeing, then it's better to either try another diet plan (or you can start monitoring your macros to find out if that helps).

Additionally, it is important to take into account that Paleo and keto aren't just diet plans which you can use to help you shed weight and optimize your wellbeing.

So as long as your daily diet follows both of these principles, you then are on the right course:

- It includes highly-satiating and well-balanced meals (protein-dense, micronutrient-rich, and/or high fiber foodstuffs).

- It limits the intake of all calorically-dense processed food items that aren't building your health.

## Placing Everything Together - The Paleo Ketogenic Diet

Honestly, you don't need to choose one diet over the other. You'll be able to stick to a ketogenic diet plan while implementing a number of the major concepts from the Paleo diet plan to enable you to obtain the great things about ketosis and Paleo consumption.

You can do this by following keto macronutrient percentages (carbs, fats, and protein) while also removing all food stuffs that aren't Paleo-approved. With regards to food options, keto and Paleo are usually, therefore, comparable that you merely have to make one change to obtain the advantages of both: remove the dairy products.

If you wish to reap the advantages of ketones and restrict the use of a dairy products for just about any cause, you might look for a Paleo keto diet plan to function as the smartest choice for you.

## *The Main Takeaway Element - What's The Best Diet Plan For You?*

Whether you choose to follow the Paleo diet plan, the keto diet plan, the Paleo keto diet plan, or even any method of feeding, you need to keep these two diet plan facts at heart:

- No diet plan is most beneficial for everyone. Because people see a positive outcome with one diet method does not suggest it's the greatest diet plan for you personally. You might have to undergo some testing before you decide to find out a diet program that can help you achieve all your targets.

53

- The main element to weight reduction is a calorie deficit. It is difficult to produce a conclusive declaration about anything concerning diet. Still, we can state a significant factor for some in line with series of researches: calories from fat will be the many essential adjustable with regards to weight reduction. To lose excess weight, you must adhere to a diet plan which allows you to maintain a caloric shortage. Whether it's reduced carb, zero fat, vegan, or perhaps a 100% all meats diet plan, a calorie shortfall may be essential to weight reduction.

In common, your daily diet should help you to:

- Accomplish a sound body structure.

- Improve your wellbeing

- Take pleasure in existence towards the fullest.

And, most of all, your daily diet should help you to sustain

54

almost all the above listed three extensively.

# CHAPTER 5

## Seven Sweeteners Which Are

## Paleo-Friendly

The paleo diet plan subscribes to the fact that we ought to eat like our ancestors. If something was struggling to become accessed by way of a caveman since it wasn't regularly happening, we shouldn't stop eating it either. This means that nearly all paleo diet plan is targeted on unprocessed, unrefined, non-packaged food items. This can consist of meats, veggies, eggs, plus some fruits and nuts. Nevertheless, this eliminates milk products, grains, and sugar.

While attempting to avoid a few of these items could be quick (think dairy-free alternatives), sugar or sweeteners certainly are a part of a wide variety of foods, including items that are marketed as healthy. If you want that sweet component, these seven paleo-friendly choices can help.

### Jerusalem Artichoke Syrup

Jerusalem Artichoke Syrup is lower around the glycemic catalog scale, rendering it useful both for all those within the Paleo diet plan and diabetics. It is abundant with a pre-biotic known as inulin. Inulin functions in you to feed some other probiotics, helping enhance the organic flora of one's intestinal tract.

### Lucuma Powder

Lucuma powder is manufactured by drying and powdering a lucuma fruit, in Peru and Ecuador. It is quite nice and pays when put into flours or additional dry goods.

### Monk Fruit

Also called Luo Han Guo, this plant native to Southeast

Asia is zero-carb and calorie, and several occasions sweeter than sugar. There's research displaying that monk fruits have antioxidant qualities, although it isn't yet known if the sweetener possesses precisely the same advantages as the entire fruit. You can buy monk fruit, natural powder or sweetener from a variety of wellness food shops or buy entire dried fruit and grind it yourself.

## Raw Honey

Raw honey is known to always be a superfood due to the several benefits it offers. It can, nevertheless, be quite saturated in carbs and calorie consumption, so it's better to utilize this sparingly as a delicacy. Additionally, it is twice as lovely as regular desk sugar, so keep that at heart when including it in some food or drink.

## Natural Maple Sap

The pure sap given from maple trees is a natural sweetener

that is utilized by Natives for years. It is solid, sticky, and contains a hint of sweetness. When boiled down and permitted to decrease significantly, it gets maple syrup. The syrup or sap could be added to quality recipes to include sweetness and rich maple flavor.

## Stevia

The dried leaves from the Stevia Rebaudiana herb, native to SOUTH USA, are an organic sweetener. They're around 10-15 periods sweeter than regular table sugar. You can buy stevia with flower, dried results in mass, or like a powder.

## Yacón Syrup

This syrup originates from the tuberous roots of the yaón plant, native to SOUTH USA. It includes a pleasant taste, much like caramelized sugar, and is particularly low in calorie consumption and carbohydrates. There's currently no business regular for yacón syrup, so you might discover that some are usually over-processed or prepared and have a higher degree of carbs

# CHAPTER 6

## Homemade Healthy Espresso Creamer

Homemade Healthy Espresso Creamer Recipe (Paleo & Vegan)! A 4 component, an easy formula that's healthier than store-bought creamers!

I anticipate the warm embrace of the good mug 'o joe each morning in my breakfast. I do like a taste of sweetness and creaminess in my espresso, though (sorry to all or any black espresso purists)! That's where this Homemade Healthy Espresso Creamer will come in!

I used to make use of store-bought non-dairy creamer. Nevertheless, one early morning I poured some into my glass; it also "glopped" into my espresso. Yes, I used the term glopped because I can't think about an easier way to spell it out it! I had been completely freaked out.

The creamer doesn't expire (I purchased it few days ago!), also it didn't have a funky smell. But it has been heavy and gelatinous, thus not natural! That has been the ultimate straw! I used to decide to make my very own dairy-free creamer that tasted incredible but experienced no chemical substances or strange "gloppy" properties.

If you're a creamer consumer like me, you'll love that Paleo Vanilla Espresso Creamer is merely slightly peculiar but adds an excellent, in-depth, organic, vanilla flavor to your coffee!

### How Will You Make Healthy Espresso Creamer?

Let's walk with the steps to make this healthful vanilla espresso creamer!

**Warm & Whisk components.** Producing coconut dairy espresso creamer is super simple! Simply place the elements (aside from vanilla coffee beans) right into a little saucepan and whisk to mix.

**View it carefully.** Next, check the mixture until it simply starts to boil, after that remove the skillet from heat. Be careful not to allow it to boil, since it can lead to a big clutter!

**Include the vanilla bean seed products and pods.** Next, scrape the seed products and mix them into the hot paleo espresso creamer mixture. Add the complete vanilla bean pods.

**Cover & allow flavors to blend.** Following the vanilla, coffee beans and pods are usually added, cover up the container, and let it sit for thirty minutes for the vanilla bean taste to infuse into the healthy espresso creamer essentially.

**Strain & shop.** Select a large cup jar and spot a-okay mesh steel sieve over it. Stress the vanilla espresso creamer into the jar and discard the vanilla bean pods.

## *How Will You Remove The Seed Products From The Vanilla Bean Pod?*

To eliminate the seeds from the vanilla bean, follow these instructions:

- Slice the bean in two.

- Carefully slice each little bit of the vanilla bean lengthwise with an extremely sharp knife.

- Use a little spoon and scrape out the seed products in the bean.

- Mix the spoon using the vanilla seed products in the espresso creamer blend and do it again with the rest of the pod pieces!

## What If I Take Advantage Of Vanilla Extract Rather Than Vanilla Beans?

If you are using a vanilla extract rather than vanilla coffee beans, I nevertheless recommend gently warming of the substances and whisking them before the combination is smooth.

However, if you are using vanilla extract, you certainly do not need to make use of a strainer or allow the mixture to take a seat on the stovetop for thirty minutes to infuse! Just whisk it in!

## Homemade Healthy Espresso Creamer

### Leap to Recipe

Homemade Healthy Espresso Creamer Recipe (Paleo & Vegan)! A 4 component, an easy formula that's healthier than store-bought creamers!

Front side view of healthful espresso creamer being

poured right into a mug of coffee.

The good friend as soon as I thought, "consuming tea is similar to obtaining a friendly handshake, but consuming coffee is similar to obtaining a warm hug." It's thus so true.

## Do you prefer coconut milk to coffee creamer?

Absolutely! We make use of coconut dairy or coconut lotion in this formula, and it works out to be incredibly creamy and super delicious! Coconut dairy is the best base for espresso creamer!

## How will you store healthy espresso creamer?

**Keep in the refrigerator.** If you intend to deploy it within a week, store it in an airtight cup container in the refrigerator.

**In the freezer.** I frequently freeze this healthful espresso creamer so that it lasts longer. To get this done, I would recommend pouring the espresso creamer into a snow cube holder and freezing it into cubes. You'll be able to simply remove a couple of cubes at the same time for you to use it early in the morning espresso! I do recommend warming the freezing vanilla espresso creamer in the microwave in your espresso mug before incorporating the espresso.

## *Paleo vanilla espresso creamer: components & substitutions*

As always, I would recommend making this formula just as written! But here are some substitutions which are possible!

**Coconut whole milk:** For a straight creamier result, make use of full-fat coconut lotion. I do not advocate changing the coconut dairy with any non-dairy milk, since it gets the highest fat content and can be an important element of this recipe!

**Almond milk.** The almond milk is put into this recipe to make sure that it doesn't solidify when stored to keep it nice and smooth. In cases like this, any other non-dairy milk may be used instead of almond milk.

**Coconut sugars:** Maple syrup or honey can be utilized instead of some or all the coconut sugar.

**Vanilla coffee beans:** I've something for vanilla coffee beans. When I wish to make a thing that isn't chocolates, not that I want it to be rich in flavor. I believe vanilla coffee beans impart a level of taste that can't be found in regular vanilla draw out. I create vanilla bean cheesecake, vanilla bean glaciers cream, and right now…vanilla bean coconut whole milk coffee creamer.

# CHAPTER 7

## Paleo and Yogurt Options

Many that are practicing the paleo diet plan are eliminating dairy but want the yogurt fix. Fortunately, nowadays, there are innovative yogurt options, a lot of which may also be befitting vegans and the ones with lactose intolerance.

**What are the health advantages of traditional yogurts?**

Conventional dairy yogurts are documented to have many health advantages:

- Saturated in protein

- Help with weight reduction

- Could be good for bone tissue health

- Can strengthen your disease fighting capability

- Abundant with nutrients

- Could help to safeguard your heart

- Aids digestive function (through probiotics)

Even though the paleo community is divided into the pros and cons of dairy consumption, if you're on the paleo diet, you might wish to choose a paleo yogurt substitute that may offer access to a number of the same benefits. We've provided some choices below.

### *Coconut yogurt*

A popular option to yogurt made out of coconut dairy, coconut yogurt includes precisely the same active cultures you discover in the dairy products variety. Coconut yogurt will be rich and creamy, meaning it's a fantastic choice for those who are seeking a kind of yogurt you could include in tested recipes. It also offers lots of the same nutrients and vitamins which are within dairy-based yogurts. As you'd anticipate, coconut yogurt consists of a unique coconut flavor that may repel anyone who isn't a lover of the fruits. It also offers slightly fewer proteins than dairy-based or soy yogurts.

## *Soy yogurt*

The yogurt alternative that's commonly loved by vegans, soy yogurt is manufactured out of soy whole milk and resembles dairy products yogurts both in taste and consistency. You can purchase this sort of yogurt in lots of stores, but many individuals choose to ensure that they have it readily at home. Soy is reasonably a common allergen; therefore you must take this under consideration before you decide to incorporate soy yogurt into your daily diet.

### *Arrowroot yogurt*

Arrowroot powder is a grain-free, gluten-free, paleo-friendly component that has several health advantages, including high degrees of metal, Supplement B and potassium, and the capability to stimulate your disease fighting capability. Made from a combined mix of floor arrowroot, probiotics, along with a solid fruits puree, arrowroot yogurt is fantastic for anybody buying paleo yogurt. You must note, however, that type of yogurt supplies a completely different gastronomic encounter than dairy types. It may possess a grittier consistency and taste more of grain or fruits than dairy.

### *Almond yogurt*

Like coconut yogurt, almond yogurt has fewer proteins

than dairy products or soy yogurts. It's ideal for individuals pursuing paleo, gluten-free, or vegan diet programs, and will have a natural, creamy texture, and a sweet flavor. Though it doesn't possess the same probiotics and energetic ethnicities as yogurt, it's a wholesome alternative that provides a number of great things about almonds, from additional nutrition, antioxidants, and nutritional vitamins to lower blood circulation pressure and cholesterol amounts.

### *Rice yogurt*

Made from grain milk, grain yogurt gets the same actives cultures as dairy products yogurt, supplying a mild taste that needs to be ideal for all palates. Because it's very much thinner than dairy products or soy yogurt, it's likely not a good option like most dairy products or soy yogurt alternatives in dishes. Still, if you're buying a simple alternative, that may be eaten alone, it's an excellent paleo yogurt choice.

## *Kefir*

Kefir- a fermented, cultured milk drink-is created from kefir grains and cow's milk, though it can be made out of coconut milk or sheep/goat milk. Because it includes a dairy products component, kefir isn't purely a paleo yogurt, but numerous paleo experts assistance incorporating kefir into your daily diet due to the wide variety of probiotic microorganisms, vitamins, and nutrients that it offers. Offering results for both bone tissue and gut wellness, kefir is a superb "not-quite-paleo" yogurt option.

## *Chia pudding*

Although it doesn't taste like traditional dairy products, chia pudding nevertheless contains lots of probiotics and omega-3s, which make it a wholesome alternative option because of chia seed products. Plus, it's an easy task to make at home. All you have to do will be soak the seed products in water, fruit juice, or non-dairy whole milk (almond, coconut, etc.), include spices, fruit, nut butter, or various other flavorings, refrigerate it overnight, and serve. Ideal for individuals adhering to gluten-free or vegan diet plans, in addition to paleo-friendly types, chia pudding is a perfect choice for breakfast or perhaps a treat between meals.

# CHAPTER 8

## 20 Paleo Breakfast Recipes

The paleo diet plan targets unprocessed foods and avoids milk products. This means your paleo breakfasts could be high in dietary fiber, with seeds, nut products, and fruits. They can furthermore offer you an early morning dose of proteins via meats and eggs. Consider these paleo breakfasts everyday recipes when you wish to start your day with nutrition-packed paleo foods.

### 1. Chocolates Coconut Granola

Paleo dieters may love this particular granola recipe each day with almond or even hemp milk, or even as a treat throughout the day. It's filled with fiber because of the almonds, coconut, and pumpkin seed products. One glass of pumpkin seed products has almost 8 grams of fiber. This recipe furthermore demands chia seed products, which have become nutritious. They're abundant in protein, fiber, calcium mineral, metal, and phosphorous.

## 2. Broccoli, Mushroom & Egg Muffins

You don't need traditional muffin ingredients to create a thing that both appear like a muffin, and hits the same place. These breakfast muffins are usually egg and vegetable-based but are often baked in a muffin tin like their grainy brethren.

## 3. Strawberry Doughnuts

With heavily processed wheat flour and sugary additives, the final treat you'd be prepared to eat on the paleo diet is a doughnut. But doughnut enthusiasts, rejoice! Here's a paleo doughnut formula for you personally. It utilizes coconut flour at the dough and freeze-dried strawberries designed to resemble red icing.

### 4. Almond Zucchini Bread

Zucchini bread is a good method to sneak vegetables onto the plates of picky eaters. With this formula, the classic cooked food goes paleo with surface almonds like a foundation. The almond flour keeps the bread collectively, just as whole wheat flour will in traditional formulas. This paleo-friendly ingredient furthermore offers a nutty taste and a nice crunch.

### 5. Sweet Potato Hash

It might seem like hash browns being a greasy diner staple. With this particular recipe, it is possible to enjoy this heavy breakfast meal without the vacant calories. The sweet potatoes listed here are shredded in a meals processor and gently sautéed in lard. Fill up the food with eggs to include a little bit of protein.

## 6. Almond & Blueberry Muffins

There are grounds why blueberry muffins certainly are a breakfast time staple. These densely tasty muffins are an easy task to get and eat the run, and ideal with very hot java or green tea. New berries will keep their shape much better than iced ones, but experience free to make use of either.

## 7. Defense Booster Orange Smoothie

When you're searching for immune-boosting vitamin A, look for meals that are well-lit orange, red, and yellow. This formula includes lovely potato, one of the better sources of supplement A. Reward factors: this morning meal smoothie can be vegan friendly.

## 8. Vintage Banana Pancakes

There's no daily breakfast menu without pancakes, however, the traditional non-Paleo variety doesn't provide much in the form of nutrition. We discovered these banana pancakes to be an easy task to create and filled with all the nutrition bananas provide, specifically, dietary fiber, potassium, and supplement C, and eggs, offering the right quantity of protein. Function having paleo-friendly fruit or maple syrup, which gives metal, magnesium, and calcium mineral.

## 9. Sausage Frittata

Savory sausage mixes with eggs and special potato with this paleo-friendly breakfast formula. You won't skip the parmesan cheese typically in a regular frittata. The shredded sugary potato offers a light mozzarella cheese (not forgetting plenty of dietary fiber).

## 10. Hawaiian Loco Moco

Here's the paleo edition of loco moco, the original Hawaiian comfort foods of white grain and meat. This recipe depends greatly on cauliflower. When prepared, cauliflower offers phosphorous, supplement C, and folate. Also, it has doubly dietary fiber as white grain.

## 11. Hazelnut Dark chocolate Crepes

The French aren't known for their paleo-friendly desserts. Luckily, there's a recipe for any paleo edition of an extremely French deal with crepes. This yummy, grain-free concoction depends on natural plantains like a base.

*Best tip: A cup of plantains provides more than 700 milligrams of potassium, which helps the body build up muscle and protein.*

## 12. Pumpkin Spice Muffins

By using full-fat coconut whole milk in these muffins, you've got yourself a moist, delicious early morning treat. Pumpkin pie spice is mainly cinnamon and nutmeg. Several studies recommend cinnamon which functions as being an anti-inflammatory and cholesterol-lowering real estate agent. Pumpkin is a superb source of supplement A.

## 13. Lovely Potato Waffle Morning meal Sandwich

Sometimes you intend to get a pub for breakfast while you run out through the entranceway, and sometimes you will need complete, filling dinner right at the beginning of the day. This recipe is perfect for the second option, craving. The minor sweetness from the sweet potatoes offers a tasty bottom for savory bacon and garlic mayo. Avocados, tomato, and lettuce get this to complete food at any moment.

*Best tip: Feel good to use yams as an alternative for sweet potatoes.*

## 14. Oatmeal

Because the paleo diet doesn't allow grains, eliminating all oats may be the only solution to create a paleo version of oatmeal. But don't be concerned, it's much less impossible since it's noise. This recipe utilizes coconut flakes and coconut flour to reproduce that grainy oatmeal structure.

*Top tip: You can include an egg to improve protein or decide on a banana to help make the formula completely vegan-friendly.*

## 15. Blueberry Breakfast everyday Cookies

If getting the kids to consume a healthy dinner before they leave for their daily activities is a problem, here's the formula for you personally. These breakfast biscuits are rich resources of nutrition, which are easy to provide when you're on the run. The combined dietary fiber from your nuts in this recipe quantities to almost 20 grams.

## 16. Sausage Egg Muffins

These bright natural "muffins" are not the sugary, fat-laden, bleached flour pastry you grab in the coffee shop. Depending on slightly almond and coconut flour to carry them together, they are protein-packed single-serving full meals. The formula can make 14 muffins altogether.

*Top tip: 2 muffins are good for one individual. Consider increasing the formula when helping large groups.*

## 17. Strawberry Pancakes

Here's the fruity, paleo formula that all pancake fans can take pleasure in. This recipe provides tasty pureed strawberries to its almond flour-based batter. A tablespoon of terrain flaxseed offers omega-3 essential fatty acids and 2 grams of fiber.

## 18. Breakfast Casserole

Busy times demand fast recipes, and hectic lifestyles demand plenty of protein. Here's a one-dish food that satisfies both requirements. Eggs are usually among nature's best protein sources. Also, they are a significant way to obtain folate and supplement D. Special potatoes offer yummy bright color and even offer more fiber and fewer calories than whitened potatoes.

## 19. Banana Bread

This recipe is a paleo and gluten-free-friendly version of

the classic comfort food: banana bread. The sweetener with this formula does its component to make a higher nutritional user profile. One-quarter mug of maple syrup has a comparable number of calorie consumption as white glucose, but it's package is an important nutrients like calcium, metal, and potassium.

## 20. Cranberry Orange Muffins

It is possible never to fail using a batch of warm, fresh muffins for breakfast. These might seem like your typical muffins, but there's a key ingredient, a superfood, in this paleo formula - avocados! They put in a creamy, damp consistency to these morning meal baked products, without interfering using the tart tastes of orange and cranberry.

# CHAPTER 9

## What Nut Butters Are Paleo? Helpful Information To Yumbutter's Potions

If you follow a Paleo way of life, the conflicting home elevators that enthusiasts of butter are allowed which could be confusing. Sufficient reason for new types of enthusiast butter developing frequently, it's not merely a query of peanut butter versus almond butter. Is enthusiast butter usually paleo? What components come in Yumbutter's potions?

### Non-seed/Enthusiast Ingredients

These potions include elements beyond nut products, but luckily, the vast majority of them are paleo! Instead of processed sugars, we make use of coconut glucose, which is paleo-approved because it originates from a herb. The same applies to essential oil. The hemp seed products and chia seed products in our superfood potions are usually permitted in reasonable quantities for paleo-eaters, and goji fruits may also be a proceed!

## Almond Butter

Well-known in the local paleo community, almond butter will be an excellent choice if you are paleo. Walnuts, along with other nut products, are usually motivated as resources of healthful fat and proteins.

## Sunflower Seeds Butter

Seed products get the paleo press in average quantities; this means sunflower seeds butter is good to go for!

## Cashew Butter

Like almonds, cashews may also be allowed in moderation around the paleo diet plan.

## Herb Proteins + Probiotic Almond Butter

This one is a bit murkier. Although walnuts are usually authorized, some paleo people choose to prevent prepared protein powders completely. If an entire body can't tolerate particular whole meals protein or you will need another protein resource, your very best wager is a sprouted, plant-based protein with several artificially prepared substances as you possibly can. Our Proteins + Probiotic Almond Butter utilizes sprouted brownish grain proteins to improve the bioavailability of the proteins and nutrition in the dark brown grain. Therefore if you are not attempting to prevent the entire protein powders, this may be a good choice. Yes, which means our Peanut Butter and Chocolates Coffee PB are usually both no-gos. Since nuts are often theoretically dried beans - which are usually ruled out from the paleo diet plan - peanut butter may be the one portion you can expect that's purely off limitations for paleo. Fortunately, with a great many other choices obtainable, you will possibly not skip it!

# CHAPTER 10

## The Very Best 10 Healthiest Food Items On The Planet (And How Exactly To Eat Them)

Consuming healthy foods offers tons of good advantages for your body and your brain. Whenever we consume nicely we sense good, whenever we experience something good we feel happier, when we're happier we're more effective, and the beautiful period proceeds. Progressively, stores and dining places all over the world are usually obtainable within the healthful consuming bandwagon, rendering it simpler for people to deal with their health correctly. This set of ten from the healthiest food items on the planet gives way to realize the fundamental minerals and vitamins the body requires to keep working at its optimum. And mainly because of an extra increase, these well-balanced meals are delicious!

## 1. SPINACH

This nutrient-dense green superfood is readily available, fresh, frozen as well as canned. Among the healthiest meals on earth, spinach will be filled with power while lower in calorie consumption, and Supplement A, Supplement E, and essential folate.

## 2. DARK BEANS

This is filled up with extremely healthful antioxidants, black color coffee beans break down slowly - maintaining your experience for longer period of time. These little special gems are usually full of calcium mineral, proteins, and dietary fiber, and their flavor is excellent!

## 3. WALNUTS

With an increase of antioxidants than any nut, walnuts may also be brimming with Vitamin E antioxidant, and abundant with herb serums, omega 3 oils, and healthy fats.

## 4. BEETS

Great for the mind and skilled in decreasing blood circulation pressure, beet is frequently ignored among the healthiest food items on the planet. The brightly-colored veggie will be filled up with folate, magnesium, and Supplement Chemical.

## 5. AVOCADO

Consuming a few avocados weekly provides you with all the good things about healthy monounsaturated fat, Supplement W6, and plenty of folates. Consult with your nearby grocer to learn when these spreadable fruits will be available in a time of year locally.

*Notice: On bread toasted with sodium and pepper, or*

*perhaps a slice of cheese if you're this way inclined.*

## 6. BLACK CHOCOLATE

Following the current study, chocolates consist of a lot more anti-oxidants, gram-for-gram, than the majority of fruit drinks – a piece of excellent news about chocoholics! Together with safeguarding your body from illnesses and assisting in preventing coronary heart problems, chocolates will be an organic mood-booster.

*Suggestion: Eat this balanced diet in moderation - just a few squares each day will do a lot of huge benefits.*

## 7. RASPBERRIES

Like the majority of berries, raspberries are filled up with antioxidants, to keep your body healthy and free from disease. New or freezing, they also offer Supplement D, calcium mineral, and metal.

*Suggestion: Spread them on yogurt or even porridge each day to start your day in an excellent and great tasting method.*

## 8. GARLIC

This pungent bulb continues to be used to defend against the illness for years, since it inhibits the growth of bacteria, lowers cholesterol, and blood circulation pressure, and contains some anti-inflammatory severe power.

## 9. LEMONS

Frequently recommended because the world's healthiest food, lemons have strong anti-inflammatory qualities and may help inhibit the development of malignancy cells. This is also as much as Supplement G as grapefruits.

*Suggestion: Put in a slice of lime in your green tea or start drinking water to get healthy and get hydrated at the same time.*

## 10. LENTILS

Finally, this mighty legume is saturated in fiber and proteins and gives excellent flavor and consistency to any meal. Vegans and vegetarians tend to be a lover of making use of lentils like a meats alternative in conventional quality recipes.

*Suggestion: Increase salads, sauces, and stews for a few additional pizazz.*

# CHAPTER 11

## 17 Healthy Paleo Snack Foods That'll Cause You To Forget You're On The Diet Plan

Who has ever thought that feeding on a caveman would become popular?

Enter the Paleo diet plan.

To make it simple, Paleo promotes a diet plan that reflects that of the Rock Age. Staples of Paleo consist of meat, fruit, vegetables, and seed products - you understand, the type of meals our forefathers grazed on.

The concept here's to create things "back to basics," leaving refined and processed food items that are frequently associated with illness.

The Paleo diet plan does not merely help people avoid weird additives and chemicals which have become so common in our foods, but additionally adopts a means of eating that supports sustainable weight-loss.

**What's possibly the biggest reward of Paleo?**

**Independence of option with regards to snacking.**

Unlike this, a great many other limited diet programs on the market, Paleo supplies a ton of healthful yet tasty options that keep carefully the diet plan from ever developing dull.

There is absolutely no shortage of healthy Paleo snacks on the market. To help push this stage house, we've come up with our very own set of Paleo snack foods for individuals of most sizes and shapes. Whether you've been on Paleo for some time or are completely new to this method of consumption, there's something on this list for you personally!

Grab-and-Go Paleo Snacks

Despite well-known belief, Paleo snacks don't need a ton of prep. Yes, almost all conventional grab-and-go cost is not Paleo-friendly because of prepared elements. Having said that, there are lots of Paleo choices that is possible to function or toss collectively very quickly.

**1. Smoked cigarettes Almonds**

Beyond offering the diverse taste, almonds contain antioxidants and vitamins and will end up being paired with almost anything. If you're buying tasty pick-me-up, be sure you buy salted walnuts instead of dry-roasted, simple walnuts with numerous snackers discover bland.

If you believe almonds independently are a bit humdrum, it is possible to very literally essence them up yourself having a spices mix. Philippine and Cajun blends are usually well-known, just as cinnamon if you like something in the sweeter part. Manufacturers like *Glowing blue Gemstone* released a huge amount of off the beaten track tastes such as BBQ and spicy wasabi for research.

## 2. Pumpkin and Sunflower Seeds

Much is not been taken off from the mighty almond, pumpkin and sunflower seed products are two healthy Paleo snack foods that deserve your interest. Like seed products are usually office-friendly on the occasion that you have them pre-shelled, specifically since they're odorless and don't group as much of the crisis. Oh, rather than to say the great things about "superseeds" which includes important nutrition like dietary fiber, metal, and omega-3h.

## 3. Path Mix

If you're not large on peanuts and seed products by themselves, setting up your path blend is certainly well worth trying. Tinkering with the choices above with some dried out fruits can lead to your very own ideal mix of salty and candy. You can even toss in a few carob potato chips to create something comparable to a conventional path blend.

Remember that nuts aren't permitted under nearly all Paleo methods. Similarly, some Paleo people discourage dried out fruits credited to added sugars. Just check out the brand and make an effort to adhere to the healthiest dried out fruit which includes:

- Pomegranate

- Goji berries

102

- Cherries

- Blueberries

- Strawberries

- Blackberries

## 4. Seaweed Snacks

Seaweed snack foods certainly are a popular Paleo choice for those attempting to replace potato chips and crackers. With an excellent supply of supplement K, snackers may also take pleasure in a lot of seaweed snack foods without the sense of guilt since they're therefore reduced in calorie consumption. Furthermore, you'll find them in several tastes which include Nice And Spicy when you can deal with the warmth.

## 5. Meats Jerky

Just like meat is stereotypically connected with cavemen, it's likewise a basic piece from the Paleo diet plan. Dried-out meats snack foods like meat and turkey jerky certainly are a wonderful solution to sneak in a few proteins to your daily diet once you do not have enough time or power to prepare a full-blown dinner. Since there are some discussion regarding whether jerky will be "good" for you, moderation and selecting lower-sodium, additive-free choices can give you some satisfaction.

## 6. Vegetable Chips

Like seaweed snack foods, kale and asparagus potato chips are healthy Paleo snack foods that will help fill up the gap remaining by crispy pretzels or poker chips. But not as nutritionally thick as real veggies, they're a shockingly tasty solution to get the vegetables.

## 7. Fruits and Vegetables

It does not have more "right down to planet" than fruits and vegetables, will it?

Paleo individuals ought to be zero strangers to new cost, although some of the snack foods above could be more appetizing. Having said that, everyone should make an effort to eat some refreshing snacks every day, and the ones on Paleo are usually no exclusion.

Some portable, no-mess lovely fruits which are perfect for work include apples, bananas, and pears, which don't have to be refrigerated.

In the meantime, celery, oatmeal, and cucumber are excellent Tupperware fare you could set with sodium and pepper, white vinegar, or " lemon " juice to produce a little more palatable.

## Paleo Snack Foods That Is Possible To Prepare at Home

Searching to produce some Paleo snacks at home? Awesome - we've obtained some tested recipes you need to certainly have a look at!

Oh, yea, and a good additional reward of the snack foods is that they don't all contain meats.

Meats can be an obvious basic piece of Paleo however, many people tend to get the "caveman" idea of the diet program a little too much. Consuming meats with every food can be costly, along with the wellness issues of the use of the reddish meats, it's superior once more that moderation and testing are fundamental to Paleo. And with having said that, below are a few healthy Paleo snack foods you may make in your kitchen.

## 8. The "Ideal" Hard-Boiled Egg

Eggs arrive often in Paleo concoctions as an alternative, but could be enjoyed independently. This formula from Paleo Jump will educate you on the artwork of the hard-boiled egg and how to make these good every time.

Hard-boiled eggs certainly are a dirt and grime inexpensive way to obtain the protein you could consume for breakfast or like a mid-day treat. Minimal clutter, minimum preparation.

## 9. No-Bean Paleo Hummus

Coffee beans are usually a good enigma to numerous

Paleo individuals. Although types such as dark coffee beans are usually certainly regarded as healthful and don't consist of chemicals, they're usually left from Paleo methods. The issue with coffee beans could be greatly divided by the people at Paleo Step:

- "The primary problem with almost all beans and legumes may be negative, instead of positive: when eaten is being a staple food, they simply crowd out more nutritious foods like animal products. "

- Because of this, Paleo people on the search for bean alternatives have to get creative. Meatified's tasty hummus formula provides you protection, making use of cashews rather than coffee beans. Hummus sets with just about any natural vegetable and may become spiced upward with additional essential olive oil, a garlic clove, or paprika for additional taste.

## 10. Cauliflower Popcorn

Hammer's toe is another Paleo no-no, while its popped range.

If you're struggling to stop your favorite cinema treat, worry not!

Say goodbye to the Wheat is a guilt-free solution to appreciate that snacks taste are yearning. Cauliflower includes minimal calorie consumption as it is a typical Paleo alternative which, contrary to popular belief, produces some incredible model "snacks."

## 11. Fast and simple Guacamole

Avocados are recognized for containing healthy body fat, but perhaps for Paleo people is the creamy structure that's much like buttery, fluffy food items which are off limitations. This guacamole formula from Paleo Jump just needs a shell to mash to excellence. In the meantime, you can test with spicier pepper types if you're sensationally courageous.

## 12. Healthy Carrot Fries

Urges are usually rough, but you can likely find healthy Paleo snack foods out there right now there to fulfill them.

Just to illustrate people from France french fries.

Taters are usually just one more controversial personality with regards to Paleo. While they're "organic" and result from the dust, some critics claim and only nutrient-rich special taters or, in some instances, neither.

No issue where you stand about taters, this model fry

formula from Eat increases in size ditches the complete argument through the use of celery. While these may not be that much audio like, they're remarkably delicious. Simply be sure you give them plenty of time to get crispy and sodium them appropriately.

**Paleo Snack foods to fulfill Your Lovely Tooth**

Probably one of the most normal issues from the Paleo diet plan is the neccesity to quit traditional sweets.

The good news? It is possible to nevertheless satisfy your sugary teeth on Paleo by using some wise glucose alternatives and fruits. These dishes will educate you on precisely how!

13. No-Bake Fruits Tart

This fruit tart from Healy Eats Real ticks the boxes of an

excellent dessert for Paleo dieters.

Simply no-bake? Examine.

Zero added sugar and sweeteners? Double-check!

A combined mixture of fruits and coconut-based filler, this wealthy deal is merely about as close up as you may get to some legit slice of cake from your beloved cafe.

## 14. Guilt-Free Banana Pudding

Provided that sticking with Paleo simply means no dairy products, rich and creamy baked materials are tricky to find. Fortunately, this pudding from Paleo Grubs might help you get your repair. This formula mainly comprised of plums and eggs which may seem easy, nonetheless, it packages on some severe taste.

## 15. Paleo Zucchini Breads Bars

Talking about plums!

Paleo going on a diet means that Frankensteining jointly deserts. Having said that, your deserts don't have to seem like replicas, and these zucchini goodies from the Driven Kitchen area are usually a primary example. With this specific formula, be sure to either say goodbye to the chocolates or make use of an alternative like a carob.

## 16. Paleo Lime Bars

Solid fruit flavors such as lemon can help you replace having less sugar in your nice snacks. Meals Belief Health and fitness' orange pubs are usually fairly much near to the "actual offer," making use of darling and coconut essential oil as an alternative for conventional butter.

## 17. One Component Fruits Sorbet

Skip striking in the snow lotion store? Don't worry! My Coronary heart Beets provide us back again to fundamentals with this particular sorbet formula. This may appear as well good to be correct with just one single ingredient, but we request you to use it yourself! Getting a high-powered blender might help but is not required.

We likewise recommend the famous one component banana glaciers lotion. These formulas function as evidence that fruits could be ever-so-versatile once you learn how to proceed with it!

# CHAPTER 12

## Are Potatoes Usually Paleo? Not Necessarily, Says Specialists

You state potatoes, we point out paleo. Potato, po-tah-to jokes apart, nutritious tubers could be an important part of a balanced, paleo diet plan. Upon this high-protein regime-think plenty of meats, seafood, fruit, and vegetables-you eat what our hunter-gatherer ancestors relied on hundreds of years ago. This implies eliminating all processed food items and staying away from grains, dairy products, and legumes.

"Indeed, if potatoes are paleo, the good question and may end up being confusing because some variations of paleo carry out to permit them. For the state or strict edition from the paleo diet plan, white potatoes are often excluded, states Randy Evans, MS, R.D., and specialist of New n' Low fat, a ready-to-eat food delivery support, that focuses on paleo meals.

You might question why potatoes are restricted since they're unprocessed. One rationale is the fact that potatoes have a higher glycemic index-meaning they elevate blood sugar levels relative to their dietary benefits, Evans describes. Other variations of paleo concentrate on actual whole foods, therefore white potatoes could be consumed in moderation.

And the next reason is basically that no one understands whether potatoes have been around before hunter-gatherers, states Heidi Moretti, MS, R.D.

"A Paleolithic diet plan is dependant on the idea of foods which were eaten before agriculture. Since nobody knows exactly when people first started consuming potatoes, the solution of if potatoes theoretically classify as paleo will be unclear,"

**Now, how about the sweet potatoes front?**

"Sweet potatoes will be the just potato that's taken into consideration paleo," explains Evans. "sweet potatoes have a lower glycemic catalog so while they will have a similar level of carbs, their effect on blood sugar levels and insulin are a lot lower, which is a goal of consuming paleo."

It's interesting to notice that whitened potatoes participate in the nightshade family members, while sweet potatoes are believed area of the morning glory loved ones.

When it comes to their vitamin and nutrient content material, Evans stresses that whitened and special potatoes have comparable dietary profiles. On the other hand, sugary potatoes boast a higher level of Supplement A, plus a greater quantity of Supplement C, B6, and calcium mineral.

"White potatoes might have higher degrees of potassium and both having similar amounts for magnesium," this individual adds.

Moretti bolsters this viewpoint, commenting, "Unlike some people's values, all potatoes are usually nutritious and filled with nutrition like potassium, supplement B6, niacin, supplement C, and dietary fiber. Sweet potatoes are usually lower glycemic catalog than whitened or reddish potatoes, but this won't mean the second option are poor foods."

By the end of your day, as Moretti strains, what condition you're feeding on, that potato in is key-you don't want us to inform you baked or boiled potatoes are healthier than french fries or taking in potatoes in chip form.

If you have problems with achy joints after feeding on meals with potatoes, you likely have an uncommon level of sensitivity: "Some individuals are private to white and crimson potatoes because of the fact they are nightshade tubers," cautions Moretti.

Speak to your physician or dietitian if you believe this can be you. Speak to your zealous pals on your paleo forum if you're prepared to nix potatoes from your diet.

# CHAPTER 13

## Can the Endomorph Diet plan Help You Shed Weight?

Whether you're seeking to drop pounds or then add muscle, getting good results involves maintaining a healthy diet plan and regular physical exercise. But based on the type of your body, some diet plan and workout programs may be better than others.

When you have a higher portion of surplus fat and little muscle mass definition, you might have what is called an endomorph whole body. Some individuals with endomorphic body struggle with weight reduction. However, the main element is focusing on how your body type differs from other styles and know what things to consume and what never to consume.

# What is a good endomorph?

The classification of various body types was introduced within the 1940s by an American researcher and psychologist William Sheldon. Through his study he figured, predicated on our skeletal framework and body structure, we all possess inherited body sorts that determine whether we're leaner, heavier, or someplace in between. As a result of this inherited physique, reaching weight reduction and workout goals often needs an individualized system.

Endomorphs are thought to have an increased percentage of surplus fat with less muscle tissue. They're frequently heavier and rounder, however, not always obese. For their bodily makeup, people who have endomorphic bodies tend to be more delicate to the consumption of calories than people who have other body varieties. Endomorphs must cautiously watch their diet to make sure they don't eat more calorie consumption than they burn off. Other characteristics add a larger body and a failure to drop excess weight.

These characteristics change from the other 2 body forms: ectomorph and mesomorph. People who have an ectomorph somatotype possess higher metabolisms, this means they can eat more and get little weight. There are also smaller joints, an inferior body size, along with a narrower frame.

The mesomorph somatotype, alternatively, is among ectomorph and endomorph. They may have a more substantial skeletal framework, but a lesser percentage of surplus fat. They can usually gain muscle tissue and shed weight easily.

### What should an endomorph eat?

When you have an endomorphic whole body and you're seeking to shed weight or get muscle definition, you might think about a workout plan and diet plan that's particular to the body type.

Based on the diet's theory, endomorphs possess slower metabolisms. Because you don't burn off calories as quickly as ectomorphs and mesomorphs, extra calories will convert to excess fat. Some think you're also much less tolerable to carbs, so the greatest diet plan for your physique could be one with an increased fat and proteins intake and a lesser carbohydrate intake, like the paleo diet plan. This diet might help you drop surplus fat while maintaining your vitality up.

Good resources of fat and proteins include:

- Macadamia nuts

- Olive oil

- Beef

- Egg yolk

- Fatty fish

- Walnuts

- Cheese

You don't need to avoid carbohydrates. Carbs are usually loaded with energy. Eliminating carbs from your diet can result in sluggishness and exhaustion. If too intense, a low-carb diet plan can also result in gastrointestinal issues and ketosis. The secret is deciding on the best sort of carbs. Concentrate on complicated carbohydrates like veggies, including starchy veggies like potatoes and tubers, legumes, whole grains, and fruits.

Curb your intake of simple carbohydrates. These food types are saturated in sugars and calories, which may cause fat storage space. Simple carbohydrates consist of white bread, whitened grain, pasta, cakes, and biscuits.

The fruit is a healthy inclusion to any eating plan. If you're carb-sensitive, consume fruits in moderation. Based on the United States Council of Workout, you should adhere to this method when preparing your daily foods:

- 30% carbohydrates

- 35% protein

- 35% fat

Portion control can be important when losing body fat being an endomorph. This can help you avoid excessive calorie consumption. Consuming 200 to 500 fewer calories from fat than you usually consume may also help you achieve your weight-loss objective.

Following proponents of the dietary plan - because endomorphs possess a harder time reducing body fat - going on a diet alone may not be enough to lose excess weight. Incorporate exercise into your day to day routine, which is a typical recommendation for anybody looking to enhance health.

An effective workout plan features a combination of a weight training exercise and cardio training.

**What does analysis say about diet plan and physique?**

There's been little study up to now that's studied how diet plan ought to be modified predicated on somatotype to accomplish specific results.

Losing weight may look like an uphill fight when your attempts don't payback. Understanding your physique, along with the distinctive challenges confronted by endomorphs, can help you fall pounds and strike your workout goals.

Maintain a minimal intake of processed carbs, get a lot of regular exercises, and practice part control. They are all healthful behaviors recommended for many people. Keeping this routine can help you lose pounds - and keep the weight loss off.

# CHAPTER 14

## How To Sustain Your Health And Weight Reduction Following The Keto Diet Plan

If you've tried the ketogenic diet plan, no one needs to tell you that this high-fat and very-low-carb strategy is restrictive. But also for all the oatmeal, potatoes, apples, and carrots you've abandoned (not forgetting desserts, bread, grain, and pasta) in the title of the so-called keto diet plan, you might have trapped with it because you've observed improvements in your wellbeing or weight reduction.

But even though you've gotten the outcomes you want, it is time to changeover using this diet. Although some people have achievement staying on keto for a long period of their time, "the long-term study is bound," states Jill Keene, RDN, in White-colored Plains, NY. Keene suggests staying on keto for half a year maximum before reintroducing even more carbs to your daily diet. Certainly, Scott Keatley, RDN, of Keatley Healthcare Nutrition Treatment in NEW YORK, agrees: "The technology hasn't reached the stage where I'd be comfortable suggesting it like a forever diet plan,"

Transitioning from the keto diet plan has its advantages. One, the keto diet plan generally advises consuming 20 to 50 grams (g) of online carbohydrates each day. (Online carbs are overall carbs with dietary fiber subtracted.) To meet up that goal, people have to cut right out healthy resources of carbs, like whole grains, legumes, starchy veggies, fruit, & most dairy products (such as yogurt and dairy). As a result of this limitation, many people will discover they can't stick to keto for a long time. What's even more, since there is such a lengthy list of prohibited food items on keto, "long-term ketogenic diet programs can lead to dietary deficiencies," states Keene. (Dietary fiber is one which many followers flunk on.)

It'll be an adjusting period, nevertheless, you can treat it in a good way. If you reach your wellbeing or weight objective on keto after that jump back into the method you were consuming (for example a typical American diet plan, which is saturated in glucose and saturated extra fat), you'll snap back to where you began, states Alyssa Tucci, RDN, nourishment supervisor at Virtual Wellness Partners in NEW YORK. "While you transit from the ketogenic diet plan, start to gradually decrease your fats consumption while boosting your consumption of slim proteins, veggies, and wholesome carbs, like fruit, whole grains, and coffee beans," she states. White sophisticated grains and sugar should be limited.

When you should nevertheless eat the healthy fats you've become familiar with (like avocado and essential olive oil), decreasing the total amount is key, otherwise, you might wind up taking in an excessive amount of calories. You'll no more be imperiling your cholesterol by addressing a chicken white meat in butter merely to meet your fat quota, for example.

Then there are worries about if you'll put on weight when you are not on keto. It's no key that the difficult part about weight reduction is maintaining it off, states Keatley. "The main element to keeping pounds off post-keto would be to adopt a number of the healthy behaviors you developed on the dietary plan," he says.

**Three Expert Strategies for Easing from the Keto Diet**

For guidance in weaning yourself from the keto diet,

follow this professional advice for an effective transition into keto result maintenance:

### *1. Gradually increase how many carbs you take in*

You might have been keeping track of carbs constantly, and you're probably a specialist in it right now. This isn't the time to stop counting. Add yet another 10g of carbohydrates each day for the initial week, says Keene. Grab a pad of paper, and track your body weight and the method that you feel. Increase that number weekly or almost every bi-weekly based on your targets, she says.

### *2. Discover Your Desired Carb Range*

The number of carbs recommended differs for everybody and differs based on things such as your targets and activity level. Since there's no one-size-fits-all quantity, aim to make contact with several carbohydrates that enable you to consume a greater selection of foods so you "don't sense limited but can sustain your fat and experience good," states Keene. If you're uncertain of the range that will be right for you, find an authorized dietitian locally who will be able to help you meet your personal goals.

### 3. Add More Proteins to your Plate

Consider increasing low-fat proteins (such as: skinless poultry, fish, lean slashes of crimson meat), says Keatley. "This can help you to take the benefit of the thermic after-effect of food, [which may be the number of calories it requires to digest food]," Keatley says. It requires about 20 to 30% of the calories in protein to digest food, weighed against about 5 to 10% of the calories in carbs.

# 10 Foods to include in Your Dish Following the Keto Diet

Next, you can strategize what you'll put back in. Listed below are 10 well-balanced meals to start including on your keto maintenance program:

## *1. Strawberries*

You might have had the opportunity to get away with feeding on a very bit (we're speaking of ¼ cup) of berries, such as, strawberries to get your fruit fix on keto. You will eat enough to make a genuine snack. One glass of strawberry halves consists of 12g of carbs, alongside 3g of dietary fiber (12% from the daily worth) and 89.4mg of vitamin C (149 % DV).

## *2. Child Carrots (or Any Carrots, for example!)*

This vitamin A-rich finger food is ideal for dipping into hummus. Ten child carrots contain 12 g of carbs.

### 3. Dark Bean Soup

A ½-cup has 10g of carbs. Best with diced avocado. Not a lover of soup? Simple, cooked black coffee beans will also grately be of help!

### 4. Edamame

When next you grab sushi, don't be timid about ordering these soybeans being an app. Two-thirds of the mug of shelled edamame offers 11g of carbs. Not forgetting, edamame can be loaded with fiber, protein, metal, and supplement C.

### 5. Kiwi

One vitamin C-packed kiwi contains simply 12g of carbs, making kiwi an ideal treat to nosh about post-keto.

### 6. Butternut Squash

Once you start on the keto trip, may very well not have

realized that lots of forms of squash were likely from the menus. But with part control, it could be back again. ½ glass of cooked butternut squash-abundant with eyesight-friendly supplement A provides 11g of carbohydrates.

## 7. Watermelon

A brilliant hydrating fruit (it's mostly like drinking water), 1 mug of melon has about 12 g of carbs and 46 calories.

## 8. Lentils

Generally, on keto you likely quit all legumes, an unfortunate fact since they're filled with fiber. Best a salad with ¼ glass of lentils for 57 calorie consumption, 4g of proteins, 10g of carbs, and 4g of dietary fiber.

## 9. Oatmeal

On keto, you might have dabbled in "oatmeal" (it's made

out of hemp seed products, flaxseed, and chia seed products) however now it's time and energy to bring back the real thing. A ½-mug serving of prepared oatmeal provides 14grms of carbs. Choose old-fashioned or steel-cut oats for the healthiest varieties. Best having a dollop of nut butter or sliced up nut products and blueberries.

## *10. Sweet Potatoes*

A number of the final things you need to add back to your post-keto diet plan are carb-rich whole-grain bread, brown grain, and potatoes (including sweet potatoes), states Keene, because it's an easy task to a group in plenty of carbs simultaneously with these meals. One-half of the medium sweet spud has simply 57 calorie consumption, but 13g of carbs. When you include them, be sure you keep the portion of the dimension in mind.

# Acknowledgments

The Glory of this book success goes to God Almighty and my beautiful Family, Fans, Readers & well-wishers, Customers, and Friends for their endless support and encouragement.

Lightning Source UK Ltd.
Milton Keynes UK
UKHW020659140521
383712UK00006B/125

9 781954 634855